A Father and Son Talk about Life, Regrets, and Making up Lost Time

By John H. Clark III

johnclarkbooks.com

Copyright © 2015 John H. Clark III

Publishing services provided by **Archangel Ink**

ISBN: 1942761597
ISBN-13: 978-1-942761-59-4

Table of Contents

Introduction 4

Talk about Dying 11

Conversation with Dad 18

Get My Books FREE 49

A Small Favor to Ask 50

About the Author 51

Introduction

Father and son relationships can be complicated – mine certainly is. Love. Hate. Respect. Fear. Worship. Disdain. Pride. Disappointment. Happiness. Anger. Joy. Sadness. The list goes on. All those feelings and emotions have come into play at one time or another with me and my old man.

John Henry Clark Jr. was born in 1936 in a little place called Hope, Texas, in his grandmother's house. He was the youngest by eight years in a family of four girls and one boy. His dad, John Henry Sr., was a carpenter who was never home much, and never had much of anything to do with his five kids, aside from "beating the devil" out of the older three girls, according to my dad's youngest sister, Aunt Nita. He evidently toned it down by the time Nita and little Johnny came along, but the older three children apparently had a pretty rough time of it. Not that Senior didn't love his kids, but he was the provider and disciplinarian of the family, not the caregiver or the nurturer. That was the mama's job, Georgia Lou, his devoted and equally neglected wife.

That's just the way it was.

And my dad grew up to be pretty much exactly like his dad. He was a good provider for his family, always worked hard repairing offset presses and other commercial printing equipment, put food on the table, and paid the bills. He earned the money and he ruled the roost. And although our needs were always met, and we were well taken care of, the roost was otherwise completely empty, in terms of love and affection. From the outside, I'm sure we looked like an all-American family – mom and dad, three kids, two dogs, Chevy sedan parked in the driveway. Inside that little 1,100-square-foot house, however, was a different story. The only times I ever saw my parents touch each other was when my dad left for work in the mornings. He would stop at the front door, turn around, lean over and kiss my mama goodbye. A little peck on the lips, and that was it. They never held hands, or sat and snuggled on the sofa, or laughed together, or said 'I love you,' or anything like that – not that I ever heard or saw, anyway.

When it came to the kids – my brother the youngest, sister in the middle and me – he was basically a tyrant, a dictator. Those terms may be a tad strong, but with my dad, what he said was law. No questions asked. Certainly there was no talking back. No talking about much of anything, really. But for us that was normal. We didn't know anything different. We weren't unhappy kids. We had friends and played outside all day long, rode the bus to school, made good grades, and mostly behaved. All that stuff. There were lots of spankings in our household – leather belt lashings, actually – mostly endured by my highly mischievous little brother, but those usually came from mama. She was the disciplinarian in the family. I'm not sure where she got the idea of using a belt, but she sure knew how to use one. According to mama's older sister, Virginia, they never got belt whippings when they were growing up, but my grandfather did draw blood once when he used a metal fly swatter on the back of her legs.

But I digress ...

Like a lot of boys, my daddy was my hero when I was young. He was a big guy, tall, strong, and he could fix things and build stuff, but I was a little scared of him. He never hurt me physically that I can remember, but he was definitely intimidating. There's a picture of him sitting in a recliner, holding me high in the air when I was a baby, but I don't remember him ever hugging me or tucking me into bed or wiping my tears or telling me he loved me or that he was proud of me – not ever. Like he says about his dad, it just wasn't done.

That's just the way it was.

When I hit my teenage years and started finding a mind of my own, things started to get a little rocky in the Clark household on Thornwall Street, down the block from Langwood Park in northwest Houston. The old man was used to strict obedience and control. Once I figured out that I really didn't have to do whatever he said, sparks began to fly. He first started to fall off his pedestal when I was 12 years old, and after I ran away from home when I was 15 (the old man tried to ground me for something I thought was completely unreasonable so I jumped out my bedroom window that night and walked probably five miles or so to the house of a friend, whose mom promptly called my parents and told them where I was), things went downhill pretty fast. By the time I graduated from high school and moved in with some friends a couple months before my 18th birthday, both my parents were glad to see me leave, so there would at least be some peace in the house.

I got married a year later and my parents got divorced a few years after that. My dad went into a tailspin of depression that lasted a long time, and I didn't feel one bit sorry for him. I thought he basically got what he deserved, and that his moping around all the time, holing up in his rundown house surrounded by growing piles of empty pizza boxes, was basically just a sympathy ploy. A woe is me sort of thing.

Then, he met a saint of a woman named Deanna. Both of them were damaged goods, and somehow drawn together like magnets. She had three sons, and watching her interact with them, so I'm told, he slowly began to learn how to communicate a little better. He sought treatment for his depression, learned how to be more affectionate, and eventually how to say, 'I love you.' I still wasn't completely buying it and in fact resented the whole transformation.

"Where was this shit when I was a little kid and needed a hug?" was my attitude.

But now, my old man really is an old man. And he's sick. He has serious heart problems and other issues, he's 78 years old, and who knows how much time he has left. Deanna sent me a text message one Saturday afternoon, and said something to the effect of, "Your daddy's not doing very well. If you want to get his stories down on tape, you might want to think about doing it pretty soon."

My dad had been saying for awhile that he wanted to record his childhood stories for posterity. He even bought one of those voice-activated word-processing programs for his computer, but apparently couldn't figure out how to get it working right. I told him I'd get down there some day and interview him and help him out. Apparently, the time was now.

I asked Deanna in a return text message to tell me straight out if my dad was dying. She wouldn't say yes or no. She just said some things about upcoming doctor appointments, and enjoying whatever time they had left together, whether it was a week, a month, six months, or 10 years. Sigh … it didn't sound good.

All I could think about was a phone call I got about 15 years ago, this one from my sister, who was telling me that my mother was in the hospital and doctors had discovered a "mass" on her brain. That was a shock to the system, naturally, but I quickly found a way to deal with it – denial.

I spent the next year pretending that my mother was not going to die. She and I never once talked about it. In fact, she told me right away that what they had found was no big deal, it was the size of a pea, and they were going to remove it and she was going to be fine, so not to worry. That sounded great. Other things she said and did as time went on raised my suspicions – like her adamantly insisting on a family camping trip that summer at Galveston Island State Park; and all of a sudden getting her will and other legal affairs in order, including having me sign some papers to give me medical power of attorney. Not to mention that huge, ugly, horseshoe-shaped incision closed with staples on the side of her half-shaved head that Christmas. Still, it was easier to pretend she was going to be okay, so that's what I did. I couldn't even begin to imagine that my mother was going to die, so I refused to consider it.

She did, in fact, die from her brain tumor. It was June 15, 2000, and because of my avoidance, I missed out on a year of opportunities to get to know my mother better, to get closer, have some heart-to-heart talks, tell her how much I appreciated her and how much I loved her. One Saturday, I said goodbye as she sat on her couch, and a week or two later she was unconscious in a hospital bed. The next week, she was gone, and before I could make it down to where she lived in Iola, near Bryan-College Station, she had been cremated (which is another story, altogether). Poof! That was it. Never saw her again. Never got to say goodbye.

I didn't want to make the same mistake with my dad.

So, a few days after those phone messages from Deanna, my youngest daughter and I drove down to Houston for a visit. I wanted to record his stories, and I also wanted to talk with him about dying, the way I wish I had done with my mother. I knew that would take a little finesse – asking someone how they feel about dying is not exactly a casual topic of conversation – but I've done lots of interviews with all kinds of people, so I knew what to do, how to work up to it.

This book is the result of that two-hour conversation, sitting in his living room with Deanna looking on, me on one side of the couch and my daughter on the other, Nita in the middle holding hands with both of us, and my old man in his favorite easy chair.

~~~~~~~~

Talk about Dying

Death is not something people like to think about, and certainly not something we like to talk about. I recently read a motivational-type book in which the author recommends that people routinely think about their own death and the simple truth that our time here on Earth is, in fact, limited. Thinking – and talking – about death can be a motivating factor, the author says, and can help encourage us to quit wasting time, to work diligently to achieve our goals, to be true to ourselves, and to appreciate our lives and our loved ones more.

My brother Bobby (actually a friend I've known since kindergarten and not an actual blood brother) demonstrated this concept once over breakfast at a café in downtown Galveston by holding his hands about a foot and a half apart, representing an imaginary timeline. We were talking about life and being happy, wasting time, procrastination, etc. He said to imagine the timeline contained 88 years of life. Then he moved his hands closer together, cutting the timeline by about two-thirds.

"If you live to be 88," he said, "this is how much time you have left. How much longer you gonna wait?"

He was right, and for some reason that stupid timeline demonstration made a big impression on me.

So when I found out that my dad's condition was apparently worse than I thought, or wanted to believe, it got my attention, and I decided that I didn't want to have regrets about my relationship with him. And I wanted to write about denial and avoidance and holding on to resentments, and missing the opportunity to mend fences and prevent guilt and form bonds. Maybe my writing about it would help someone else. I knew it would help me; writing is a way to help me sort things out.

"We don't like to think about death, because it's painful," says Jeffrey Robbins, a Central Texas family counselor. "And, so, avoidance can be a very strong coping mechanism. Most often, avoidance is a very bad coping mechanism. If I avoid the bill collector, he is going to come and take my car. But we want to feel good in the moment, and so we push that reality away.

"But it's best if we do think about our loved ones who are going to die, and even think about our own death. The reality of it is, the older we get, we do start to think more and more about our death, so that notion of getting your father's stories on tape ... I had a similar experience with my grandfather. He wasn't on his death bed or anything like that. He was a couple of years away from when he was dying – which we didn't know – and he started telling all of these stories and he started taping them for us. So here he is, in his 70s, and he's already starting that process of thinking about his own death and the kind of legacy he wants to leave – what information he wants the family to know.

"I have a great memory of sitting in the living room, all the grandkids are around, and we're listening to his stories as he's right there playing them," Robbins explained. "It's so cool. And when the story is done, he's turning off the recording, and we're processing it. And that is one way to kind of help family members deal with the notion of so-and-so is going to die.

"Talking about death is extremely difficult," Robbins said. "It's not an easy conversation. I've never known anybody where it's a comfortable conversation. Often times, it's very emotional. It's going to be upsetting for both people, but it's beneficial. Talking about it is helpful for both people. And people who have those conversations say that they tend to be very valuable. When we know someone is dying, and it is not talked about, when things are left unsaid, I see a lot of guilt. Things like, 'I wish I would have said this or that,' before he or she died. And it usually starts with, 'I wish I would have said how much I love them; how much I appreciate them.'

"I also encourage people to think about what it's going to be like when a family member is gone. What's it going to be like? What's it going to feel like, to be doing my routine knowing that this loved one is not going to be in my life? That's another way of preparing.

"I had a very close loved one given a diagnosis, and I took a year to prepare. It was still painful, but that was real helpful, because I had thought about what it's going to be like, and what is it going to feel like? This was '07, and I still miss the loved one dearly, but it's okay because I didn't avoid it. I knew it was going to be big. This was the biggest loss I ever had in my life, and I knew that if I didn't prepare for it, I wasn't going to cope well.

"Interestingly enough, it was my dog. This dog was the love of my life. Now, I'm not proud to say that I loved my dog more than my wife, but that's the God's honest truth. There was something special about that dog. Everybody that saw that dog, they just kind of lit up. They felt joy. That's what he brought. I still miss him dearly. I talk to him – which is a good strategy for coping with a loss. Can he hear me? I don't know. Does he talk back? No. But it's helpful.

"I tell people that grief is like a wave. It comes in on the shoreline, and we're walking along the shoreline. Some of those waves don't get anywhere close to our shoes, but every now and then, there's a big wave. And if we don't move, it's going to flood our shoes. That's what grief can feel like at times – it floods us. 'I can't breathe; I'm choking to death.' I tell people, 'Go with that grief. Feel that pain. Cry.' That's very therapeutic, very healing."

I haven't experienced a lot of death in my life. I have a vague memory of being at my grandfather's funeral – my dad's dad – when I was five years old. For some reason, I have a picture in my mind of my Aunt Nita bending over to kiss him in his casket. There was a kid at church who was hit by a car while riding his bicycle that died when I was probably about nine years old. I remember going to that incredibly sad funeral. When I was 18, a friend died in a car wreck. I went to that funeral, and it was pretty bad. My mother's dad committed suicide with a deer rifle when I was 29, and there was a closed-casket graveside service at the cemetery. I was not really close to him, and did not feel particularly sad, although I grew to miss him over time. My mother died the year I turned 43 and there was no funeral. There was a memorial service at her little country church, and I struggled to maintain my composure as I stood at the podium and read a tribute to her that I wrote. I could barely get the words to come out, but I did not cry. I thought if I allowed myself to cry that I might never stop. The last funeral I went to was my grandmother's (my mother's mother) and it was not particularly sad. Maybe because she had a good, long life, and maybe because she suffered quite a bit at the end. What I remember most about her death is watching her unconscious in the hospital, struggling mightily to breathe.

My father's mother died 35 years ago, and for some reason I don't remember anything about that, or even going to a funeral for her. My uncle Howard died recently, but there was no funeral, and I had not seen him for a number of years. He was a neat guy, but I didn't feel a lot of sadness upon hearing the news. I don't know why.

Writing all that down actually makes it sound like a lot of death. I hate death. It is so sad. But I think about it a lot more than I used to – my own death included. I have always felt dissatisfied with my life because I have not accomplished great things, because I did not reach my potential, because I made so many bad decisions and did stupid things and squandered my talents for so many years. But now, well into my 50s, I have started to let go of some of that, and think more about my legacy. And, perhaps, equally as important, I have started to utilize one of my talents, which is writing. At least I'm not wasting that one anymore. I have a strong creative side, and I love to write. It is something that truly feeds my soul, a way to express myself. I need that. And a number of years ago, I came to the conclusion that whatever I may or may not accomplish in this life, if my two daughters can honestly say – after I'm dead and gone – that I was a good dad, then my life will have been an overwhelming success. That's it. Nothing else really matters. Well, I also want to travel the world and write more books, but being a good father will be my number one accomplishment.

As for my dad, I'm certainly not looking forward to the day he dies. That is something I do not want to experience. But it is going to happen. Who knows? I may go first. And I've thought about that, too. As a matter of fact, I've already asked my friend Bobby, who is a gifted public speaker, to preside over my funeral service and deliver the eulogy.

But the odds are, I'll be attending my dad's funeral one of these days. And I want to be there with no regrets, and speak with pride about my old man. I want to get to know him better, and I want him to get to know me better.

~~~~~~

John Henry Clark Jr.

Conversation with Dad

When we got to his house that day, my daughter and I walked in the back door and nobody was around. We said, 'Hello!' and my 88-year-old Aunt Nita came walking into the room. She moved in with my dad and Deanna after my uncle Howard died. Nita and Howard were together for more than 60 years. It was never just Howard or Nita. It was always Howard and Nita. They were inseparable. Nita is a character. She loves me, and I love her very much.

When I was a kid, we spent a lot of time at Howard and Nita's house in the West University area of Houston, near the Rice University campus. We always went there for Christmas, and watched a lot of Dallas Cowboys football games on TV, including the famous 1967 NFL championship game between Green Bay and Dallas, known as the Ice Bowl for its sub-zero weather conditions. Lots of times when we visited Nita and Howard, we got to eat Whataburgers or take-out Mexican food from Monterrey House. Our family never went out to eat, so that was a real treat. And Howard, who did a world-class Donald Duck imitation, had enough cool toys to open his own store.

We all hugged and kissed and all that good stuff, and Deanna and my dad eventually came into the living room. Everybody sat down and chit-chatted about this and that, and it wasn't too long before my old man decided it was story time. So I whipped out my tape recorder, pushed the button and off he went:

When I was about two or three-years-old, we had just moved back to Houston from down Yoakum way, and my dad was fixing a screen door on the porch. To do that, you have to tack a corner, pull the screen tight and tack another corner. Well, when he would pull, he would lay his tack hammer down, and while he wasn't watching, I would pick up his tack hammer and run off with it. He would have to come find me, and I'm sure he would chastise me.

But I thought that was a pretty good game. So I had done that a half-dozen times, probably, and one time as he was working on the screen, he looked up just as I was reaching for the hammer, and he said I looked so guilty that he needed to laugh, but he didn't want to laugh with me looking at him. He figured that would make me think my little game was even more fun. So, he ducked his head to laugh and I picked up the hammer — and hit him in the head with it.

And there was an old Christmas tree laying on the porch, so he snatched a branch off of it and started switchin' my legs. I had on short pants, and I started screaming bloody murder, of course. And one of my sisters, Juanita, ran between us, and another one of my sisters, Ruth, picked me up and ran off with me. So now, we're all three in trouble.

But when he caught up with everybody — those Christmas tree needles had punctured my leg a little bit, so I had a little blood there — and he saw he had hurt his baby boy, it was all over with. He wasn't mad at anybody, anymore ... except himself.

When he was little, my dad's family lived back and forth between Hope and Yoakum, before eventually settling in Houston, where my old man went to school and graduated from Milby High. His oldest sister, Anna Lou, had 15 kids, including a daughter who is older than he is. He always talks about having a niece who is older than him. His other sisters were named Bonnie, Ruth and Nita.

I don't remember much about John Henry Sr., who died Dec. 18, 1962, when I was five. I know we called him granddaddy, and the only memories I have of him — besides the image of Nita kissing him at his funeral — are when he held my hand and led me into his kitchen, where we shared a can of Vienna sausages, and then the day I stood on the sidewalk outside St. Joseph's Hospital in downtown Houston, where he was dying from emphysema and lung cancer. I remember waving up at him as he stood in a second- or third-floor window, waving back. My dad's mother — her grandkids called her Maa-Maw — was a sweet, little old lady. I have hands like hers, with prominent veins on top that I used to call "worms," and still do, when someone notices them on me. She worked at a drug store, and died in her 70s of a massive heart attack.

John Henry Sr. and Georgia Lou Davis were married in Hope, Texas, standing in a horse-drawn buggy. All their kids were born in Yoakum or in Hope. My granddaddy worked as a carpenter, stone-cutter and sculptor, and had a job with the railroad for awhile. My dad recalls:

He could walk onto a vacant lot, and leave with a house built – except for the electric and plumbing. And he also worked for a marble yard in Yoakum. One of the stories is that he came up to Houston because a lady had contracted them to put in a mausoleum for her family. And it was supposed to be six-feet deep. Well, they got down to about five-and-a-half feet and hit bedrock, and they couldn't dig any deeper.

So they sent Daddy up to try and pacify her – she was insisting they go to six feet, because that's what they said they were going to do. So, he measured it and he said, 'You're right – I'll take care of it.' And everybody went home. The next morning, he went out there and he had one of those folding wooden rulers, and he broke six inches off of it. Then, when the lady came back out, he put the ruler in there and it was six-feet deep. It didn't hurt anything – there was no way they could dig any deeper – and she was satisfied.

And there's a tombstone in a cemetery on Washington Avenue – where I used to play all the time – that he was supposed to have designed and sculpted. It's a very beautiful thing. We'll have to go and take a picture of that sometime.

My parents' wedding in 1955, with John Henry Sr. and Georgia Lou on the left (Granddaddy and Maa-Maw); and Sybil and George Fern on the right (Grandma and Paw-Paw)

Senior was a stern, mostly unsmiling, hard-working man who was away from home a lot, either working or looking for work. If he wasn't traveling somewhere in search of a job, he was up and gone before sunrise, and usually didn't get home until late at night. He wasn't a drinker, but smoked non-filtered Camel cigarettes all his life. My dad describes their relationship as "very distant."

He was like me – like you describe me. No huggy-kissy. He wasn't a bad disciplinarian with me. That time with the switch is about the only time he bothered me, but with the first three girls, he was very stern.

Aunt Nita chimes in at this point: *He used to beat the devil out of 'em. He was so mean to them.*

Dad nods in agreement and continues:

When mama found out she was pregnant with Nita, she started crying. He said, 'What are you crying about?' She said, 'I just hate to bring another child into the world for you to pick on.' He said, 'Well, if that's a problem, they won't get any more discipline from me.' So Nita and I never were disciplined by him – except for that one time.

I wasn't afraid of him. I loved him. I remember my first recollection of my dad was in Yoakum, when I was still in a crib. I could stand up, and I think I could walk. One night, I was sleeping, and he came in. It was wintertime, and it was cold. Mama didn't want to wake me up, but he couldn't stand it – he had to wake up his boy. So he came in there and woke me up, picked me up, and I still remember his smell. He smelled like cigarettes, because he smoked a lot. That's my first memory of him. I also remember going down to the river one time with him and ... I think it was Uncle Jim. Uncle Jim was Bonnie's husband. They went down there and got several bags of sand, and Daddy built me a sandbox.

But we never did get real close. And I've always regretted that. Like me with you, I don't remember him ever telling me he loved me, and I don't remember ever telling him I loved him. I think I knew he loved me – after all, he was my provider. I think the way he showed love was by getting up before dawn and working all day.

One of the nice things that he did was when I was throwing a paper route. I first had a paper route when I was nine years old. It was during the Second World War, and I used to save my money, so I saved up my dimes and bought a $25 war bond. I was being patriotic. I had that war bond for years. Then, one year, they needed some money, and mama asked me if she could cash that war bond. I said, sure, and I forgot about it. Then, when 10 years had passed, we were sitting at the dinner table or at breakfast or something, and daddy handed me twenty-five dollars. I said, 'What's that for?' He said, 'I promised myself, when you cashed in your war bond, that when it matured, I was going to give you back your money.' I thought that was real neat.

In those days, daddies just didn't lovey-dovey with their kids. And if they didn't discipline them, the kids didn't even hardly know they were around.

My Dad as a young boy

For the first two years of his life my dad was a sickly kid. He weighed less at six months old than he did when he was born, Nita recalls, and by the time he turned two, he weighed all of 18 pounds. Today, doctors would no doubt run all kinds of expensive tests and prescribe who-knows-what kinds of medications, referrals to specialists and such, but back then, the remedy was pretty simple.

A new doctor came to town, and mama took me to him — she had already taken me to all the other doctors there in Yoakum — and he examined me and said, 'There ain't nothing wrong with this child, except he's starving to death.' So, he recommended to her, and I don't know why, that she feed me orange juice and cod liver oil. He said, 'Now, you'll probably have to hold his nose and pour the cod liver oil down his throat, 'cause he ain't going to like it at all.'

Well, I went home and showed 'em — they had to hold my nose to pour the orange juice down, and I licked the spoon on the cod liver oil. The reason we couldn't drink orange juice is because mama used to put something in it to 'clean us out' after the winter. What was it ... Castor oil, I think it was.

Another time, I had started eating dirt. Mama took me to the doctor, and he said, 'He's missing something in his diet.' She didn't know what to do about it, and he didn't, either. So, she just brought me home and tried to keep me from eating dirt. I used to go out to the cow lot with her, to milk the cow, and they had some bins with feed in it. One of the feeds they had was cotton seed meal. And I started eating that. So she took me back to the doctor.

She said, 'Now, he's eating cotton seed meal.' He said, 'Well, it's better for him than dirt.' To this day, if I go into a feed store and smell that feed, my mouth waters.

I don't have many early childhood memories like that, from when I was a little-bitty kid. I remember that scene from my granddaddy's funeral, the Vienna sausages and waving up at him in the hospital, and I can remember one time riding a skateboard down the driveway on my stomach, weaving back and forth through some kind of tin-can obstacle course we had laid out. My dad tells about the time when I was about as tall as a car bumper, and I took an axe out of the garage and started whacking a fender on his brand new car with it. I don't remember doing that. I've seen a photograph of him mowing our front yard on Thornwall Street, with me "helping" push the mower, but I don't remember that, either.

The first memories I have with my father, meanwhile, are when I was between eight and 14, and start with Little League baseball and peewee football, which is where we spent most of our time together, either going to practice, going to games, him going to announce games or keep score, me going to hang out with my friends and watch games. Once he took me with him to cut the football field grass. I got to drive the riding lawnmower and at one point I ran into the goal post at one end of the field and broke the steering on the mower. I imagine he got pissed, but I don't remember him yelling at me or anything. I don't remember what happened, exactly, just that I broke the mower.

My dad coached the teams I played on most of those years. He loved it. He loved it as much or maybe more than I loved playing – and I really loved it. Sports was my life when I was a kid. My old man hated to lose, and I remember him staying up late at night after baseball games, sitting at the kitchen table, going over and over the scorebook, analyzing results of the games. He would say things like, 'Winning isn't everything, it's the only thing,' quoting the legendary Green Bay Packers football coach Vince Lombardi. I took that stuff literally and died inside a little bit when we lost a game, and usually found a way to blame myself somehow, especially in baseball, and especially if I was pitching a game and we lost. Luckily, that didn't happen very often. I was a pretty intense kid and worked my butt off at sports, practiced all the time. I had a regulation pitching mound, home plate, and small backstop in the backyard – built by my dad – and I was always out there pitching one ball at a time into one of those nets with a strike zone painted on it. Throw the pitch, walk down and get the ball, walk back to the mound, throw another one, on and on, over and over. Nobody forced me to do it. I wanted to do it. That's just the way I was.

One of the stories my old man tells about my perfectionism as a kid (neurosis, maybe) and I do remember this – was the time all the kids in the neighborhood started getting sidewalk skates. These were the kind of skates they now call antiques, with metal wheels and a metal key that you turned to tighten little clamps that held the skates on your feet. Like everybody else, I got some skates, but I didn't take them outside and join in the zooming up and down sidewalks and dodging parked cars in the street. I took my new skates into our closed one-car garage and skated around and around in circles, bouncing off walls and a big, white chest freezer until I thought I was good enough to go outside.

But, again, I digress ...

By the time my dad was old enough to go to school, his dad was home most of the time, but they still rarely saw each other. When the kids got up in the morning, the old man was already gone for the day, and he didn't come back home until after they were in bed. He did not attend my dad's high school graduation – too busy with work – but did go to his wedding. It was not long after my dad married my mother that his old man started getting sick. Incapacitating emphysema came first, and eventually what was then referred to as upper respiratory cancer.

Aunt Nita blames his job as a stone cutter for the emphysema, while my dad points to a lifetime of sucking on cigarettes.

I think maybe 40 years or 50 years of smoking might have had something to do with it, too. He finally quit smoking before he passed away.

When Daddy died, I decided I was going to quit smoking. I was 26 then, and I had started when I was 15. It took me from the time he died, which was in December, until May the next year before I got quit. I would quit for a few days, then I would go back to it. I tried and tried to quit, then I decided I'd quit buying them. I figured that would work, because I'd be too ashamed to bum. But I wasn't.

When I was working for Addressograph-Multigraph, we had a four-day weekend – I think it was Memorial Day weekend – and I hadn't smoked all weekend. When I came back to work, we were back in the service department, and all the servicemen were smoking, so I bummed a cigarette. And I took a deep ol' drag on it and got dizzy. I looked at that cigarette, and I said, 'I don't need this.' And I put it down, put it out, and I haven't picked one up since.

And I know as well as I know anything that if I picked one up again, I'd be smoking a pack a day again tomorrow. I really enjoyed smoking. It's an addiction.

I quit drinking after a friend of mine came over to the house one day – we were living over there on Thornwall – and we started playing Canasta. I had a fifth of Canadian Club (whiskey) that somebody had given me for Christmas. This was in the summer time and I hadn't even opened it yet – that's how much I drank. But we opened it, and he and I started drinking. And our wives drank maybe a drink. After awhile, I went to get me some more, and it was gone. He and I had drank the whole thing. And when it started hitting me, I could tell whether the cards were black or red, but I couldn't tell what the suit was – whether they were diamonds, clubs, hearts or spades. After he left, I went and laid down, and the bed started spinning around. That was the first time I'd ever had that happen. Then, I got up and urped my guts out, and went on back to bed.

I went to work the next day, but that's when I decided I didn't need to drink anymore. Never took another drink ... until one time years later. I was out at a customer's of mine – he drank a lot – and he was always teasing me about being a Mormon and not drinking. So, I was out there working one day about quitting time, and he said, 'Why don't you come on by the house when you finish? I think I got some orange soda water!' I said, 'All right.'

So I went by his house, and he asked me what I wanted to drink. I said, 'How about a screwdriver?' So he made me a screwdriver and I drank it – he was sitting there watching me, just amazed that I was taking a drink – but by the time I finished drinking that drink, I had a big buzz on and I decided that wasn't such a good idea. So that was the last time.

My dad, being the baby of the family, spent a lot of time with his mother when he was growing up. She was baptized a Mormon when she was eight-years-old by people traveling through the New Mexico territory, my dad says, and that's how he become affiliated with the Mormon Church. After us kids were old enough, our family started going to church on Sundays and Wednesdays, but we weren't exactly what I would call devout. I used to sneak out of church all the time with my friends during Sunday school and walk down to the corner store. Then we'd go back and sit together in the back of the chapel eating candy during the morning service. I started refusing to go at all when I was about 15, and I've never been back.

But, my dad and his mother were extremely close and stayed that way even after he got married and moved across town. His dad's death was painful, but he was heartbroken when Maa-Maw had a massive heart attack and died on April 18, 1979, at age 75.

I remember one time, when we were living over almost downtown now (in Houston), I was supposed to be asleep. They told me to go to sleep, and I didn't want to go to sleep. It was about Christmas time, and mama and I were going down to Yoakum for Christmas. Daddy never did go with us. He stayed home and worked. So, they had bought me a rifle, an all-wooden rifle, with four or five triggers on it, and then it had a reed – like on a musical instrument – and that reed would snap. That was how it 'shot.' And they were talking about, 'How are we going to get this rifle down there without him knowing it?' And I sat up in bed and said, 'What rifle?'

After I was grown, I was out around town all the time on my job, working on printing equipment, and I went by mama's house a lot of times during the day, and she fed me and we talked, and that sort of thing. So, I felt a lot closer to her, but I think with my dad, I was so upset when he died because I realized that I never had that kind of relationship with him, like I did with her.

Hopefully, I'll get a chance, when I cross the veil. If my church is right – if the Mormon Church is right – I will see him again. If you are a member of the church in good standing, you can be sealed to your family for all time and eternity. So, that's a very comforting thing.

I felt a loss when my daddy died, but it wasn't as serious a loss to me, because I had a lot better relationship with my mom. I think Nita called, and said that mama had had a heart attack. I couldn't believe it. Your mama and I went over to their house, and Nita said the ambulance had taken her to the hospital – but we didn't know which hospital. So, we went to a couple of hospitals, and the whole time, I'm thinking, 'She can't be dying.'

Nita had come home from work, and mama said, 'Honey, I got the worst pain under my arm.' About that time, she just hit the floor, and Nita panicked. She called 911 and said, 'My mama's just had a heart attack, I think,' and hung up the phone.

They must have had some kind of caller ID, because the ambulance was there in 10 or 15 minutes. They worked on her for a while, but they couldn't do any good, so they took her to the hospital. I don't know if she was still alive when she got to the hospital, or not. But when I got there, they said she had passed away. I said, 'Where is she?' They said, 'She's back there.' And I said, 'I want to see her.' They said, 'You don't need to go back there.' I said, 'I'm going to see her.' I was still in denial, at that point. She couldn't have died, you know? So, I went back there, and it was a horrible sight. Her head was thrown back, with her mouth open, and the rigors of death ... in a way, I was sorry I went back there, but in a way, I was glad. Because it was, 'Now, I know she's dead.'

He never got a chance to say goodbye to his mom, the same way I never got to say goodbye to mine. The circumstances were a little different, though. I had ample opportunity to say goodbye to my mother, but didn't, or wasn't able to, take advantage of it. My dad had no choice, but he did get to say his goodbyes, in a way. He got to see her one last time, even though it was a sight he'd like to forget.

Like me and my mom, though, my dad missed that chance with his dad. Even with the old man on his deathbed, after being sick for several years, there wasn't much of anything said between father and son.

He was in and out of the hospital a couple of times. And so my biggest memory is, he was in the hospital – St. Joseph's in Houston. He had a tumor on his neck, and when the doctor came in to tell us about it, he said it was cancer. I said, 'Are you sure it's cancer?' He said, 'Oh, yes, it's big-time cancer.' And I thought, 'My daddy's gonna die.' And I went out on the fire escape, and I'm looking at the people down below, walking along the streets and stuff, and I thought, 'All those people ... they don't know my daddy's dying, and they don't care.' And I felt really sad. From then on, of course, I was very attentive to him.

To tell you the truth, I don't remember what he and I talked about. But we never did tell each other we loved each other – not that I remember. I don't remember me and you doing it, either, for a long time. And I think that was because of the way my daddy was with me. We do, to a great extent, follow our parents' example.

In a lot of cases, a boy marries a woman who is a lot like his mama. And a girl marries a man who is a lot like her daddy.

When he was in the hospital the last time, of course, everybody went to see him, and he told mama, 'Well, I guess all my kids do love me, after all. They all came to see me.' So, evidently, he had the same doubts that I had about you guys. I wasn't sure whether you loved me or not. But at least I'm still alive while I'm finding it out.

I was sittin' in that waiting room one day, and that young nurse that we had that was so good came by and said, 'If you want to see him, you'd better go back in there.' So we did, and he wasn't conscious or anything, but he took his last breath. I was there in the room, and I saw him take his last breath. And I leaned over and kissed him, and put my head on his chest. His heart was still beating, but he wasn't breathing any more.

I went over to Nita's house, and I just boo-hooed. I cried — big-time. Couldn't stand it, hardly. But I didn't feel until after he was gone how much I had missed ... not being close. Me and him never went fishing together. We didn't go to the movies together. We just didn't do things together. The only thing I remember is when we lived over on Jefferson Street, and we had a house that was about four feet off the ground. I think Howard was out there, and me and daddy, and they were throwing the football around. It was supposed to be all of us throwing the football around. Daddy would fake it to Howard and then throw it to me, and it would hit me. I was too young — eight or nine years old — and didn't have quick enough reflexes to catch it. I finally got to where when Daddy had the ball, I'd go hide behind the house!

I wish that I could back up time, and spend time with him. And I'm hoping that when I get there (heaven), that I'll be able to, and tell him I love him. And I'm sure he will return it.

It's only been in the last few years that my old man has learned to show affection, and tell people he loves them. And it's been even more recently that I've decided that it's okay. People can change. People are a product of their upbringing and sometimes just flat-out don't know any better.

For a long time, I blamed a lot of my problems, mistakes and stupid decisions on my dad. I blamed him for not giving me guidance as I grew up – not helping me make decisions and figure things out. We just didn't have that kind of relationship. Hell, I got married for the first time shortly before my 19th birthday because somebody hugged and kissed me and said she loved me. I imagine my mama told me she loved me when I was growing up, but I really don't remember. I know I always felt that she loved me, because she was my mama and she took care of me, brushed the dirt off my skinned knees and kissed my boo-boos. But my old man? I spent a lifetime trying to make that guy proud of me and never seemed to pull it off.

But now, he tells me he loves me and is proud of me, and I believe he really is. Part of it may be a result of him getting older and mellower, but some of it is apparently because he just never learned how to do it. And that it is important.

I guess it all started when I met Deanna. She's very lovey-dovey. I got lovey-dovey with her, and then I saw how she was with her kids, and how she brought them up. They say 'I love you' all the time. And I thought, 'I didn't do that with my kids.'

I saw how they interacted, and I wished that we had done some of that. We didn't do it when y'all were little, and it wasn't done in my family when I was little, either. Children in those days were to be seen and not heard. That's the way it was back then. After you kids got to walking and stuff, I was of the opinion that if you could walk and talk, you could sit down and shut up, too. But, because of that, I missed out on a lot with you kids, I feel like.

But, anyway, that's when I started saying, 'I love you,' after I met Deanna. In fact, sometimes I'd say it too much. Sometimes I'd be talking to somebody on the phone — a clerk at a store or something, you know — and when I'd start to hang up, I'd say, 'I love you.' I don't even know 'em!"

My stepmother, Deanna, who I resisted getting to know for about as long as I scoffed at my old man's attempts at changing his ways, remembers them both being damaged goods when they met at Raveneaux Country Club in Spring, Texas, in the summer of 1982. Deanna was a guest at the club, where her sister was a member, and my old man was working as a lifeguard. She recalls:

When I first met him, we were both traumatized — me from having my husband die, and he from his divorce. But he was very kind to me, and we found comfort with each other. It's really hard for a woman to be alone. It's very dangerous and scary. For him, I think he just needed to be loved.

But it was very hard to get through to him. He didn't want to commit to anybody, or anything, really, because he was so burned. But after a time, he finally started to be a little more trusting. And he was always so helpful. Anything that was broken, he would fix it. He would come over and bring me flowers ... trying to get close to somebody.

And then, he saw me talking and negotiating with my children. Which he didn't believe in negotiations. Whenever the boys would get cross with me, I would go and say, 'Hey, this is not working for me. And I would like to know where you're coming from, because I'm not real sure where you're coming from. It's not looking good from my view, so tell me your view.' And they would, and it was always something different from what I expected. I was always thinking the worst, and by the time I understood the why and where they were coming from, then I could understand the situation. So he watched that, and he watched me hug these boys, and [watched] them come over and tell me all the things that had happened ...

He watched fairly incredulously, I'm sure. Remember, this was before the transformation began. My dad continued the story:

I'd never seen that before. When I was a kid growing up, I didn't tell my mama everything I did.

For instance, one of Deanna's boys one time was leaving the mall and he got turned around. He got lost, and was walking down (a busy highway) before they found him. And he told his mama, 'Oh, it was so awful, and I was so scared, and ...'

When I'd do things that would upset my mom, I didn't ever tell her about it. And he always wanted to negotiate, when she wanted him to do something he didn't want to do. He'd actually say those words: 'Can we negotiate about this?' And she would negotiate with him. I couldn't believe that.

One time, when I was a young man, me and three of my buddies had been downtown – we walked everywhere we went; we didn't ride the bus because we couldn't afford to – and we were walking home. We passed the old Sam Houston Coliseum, and there was a bridge there over Buffalo Bayou. There was a bus barn across the street, just before you got to the Coliseum. And in the old days, the parking meters — of course, they weren't active at night — if you hit them real hard with your hand, time would come up on them. So we were walking along, making time come up on the parking meters. And then somebody hit one, and it broke. And somebody said, 'Hey, man, there's nickels in that thing.' So I stood it up, and I started kicking it, trying to get it loose. I found out later it was chained in there, and I could have kicked it all day. So, I'd stand it up, and I'd kick it again. Then, somebody noticed that the people over at that bus barn were watching us. So, we decided we'd better get out of there. We went and hid under the bridge, and pretty soon, we saw a cop car pass. And everybody said, 'Now, we can go.' We knew that bayou like the back of our hand, and I said, 'Why don't we go across the pipe — that went under the bridge — and into our neighborhood that way?' They said, 'Ah, no, it's all right. They already passed.' I said, 'OK, then why don't we go one at a time, so all of us won't get caught?' So, we all started across the bridge, and before we knew it, they were pulling us over, searching us and all that.

They took us downtown, and the jail then wasn't where it is now. The jail now is in that old neighborhood, but then it was on the other side of downtown. We were all sitting out in the lobby, and none of us would admit it, but all four of us were scared to death. My biggest fear was that they'd call my parents. Finally, this guy come in and he says, 'You bunch of hoodlums come on in here.' So we got up and went in there, and he said, 'Empty your pockets.' So we did, and Donald Curry had a pocketknife. The guy picked it up and opened it — and it was sharp as a razor. He said, 'What do you do with this knife, boy?' Donald said, 'I clean *my fingernails.'* The guy had a little slit in his desk that he would stick knives in and break 'em off. So he stuck that knife in there, then he said, *'Aw, never mind.'* Then he folded it up and gave it back to him.

They told us that if we got in any more trouble for the next six months or whatever that we'd really be in trouble. So we left – and, of course, after we left, we was real brave. We were talking about those S.O.B.s had brought us all the way over here, and now we had to walk all the way back. Why didn't they take us back to where they found us? All that kind of stuff.

So, when we got back over that way, where we were before, Donald was afraid to go home. He lived with his dad, and he was afraid his dad was really gonna get on his case. It was midnight by then. So I said I'd walk with him. Well, after I walked him home, that got me home about two in the morning. And my mama was standing out in the front yard. She said, *'What in the world are you doing getting home this late?'* I said, *'Well, Donald wanted to go to his mother's, and he didn't want to walk by himself, so I walked with him.'* I sure didn't tell her nothing about going to jail.

The last time I saw him, my old man was in good spirits, but a lot frailer than I'd ever seen him before. About six months earlier he was walking around pretty well. Moving slowly, but steadily. This last time, he needed someone on both sides of him, holding under each arm, for support. We went to a restaurant for dinner – Deanna, Dad and Nita in one car; my daughter and me in another car – and we parked in separate sections of the parking lot. When I walked into the outside patio area, my old man was sitting on the edge of a large fountain with his head down, slumped over. He was resting while Deanna and Nita went inside to get a table. After dinner he needed to sit and rest on the way out, too.

Basically, his heart doesn't work properly. He has a condition called atrial fibrillation, which is abnormal heart rhythms. I don't know a whole lot about it, but apparently the heartbeat rhythms can be abnormally fast or abnormally slow. He has had both kinds – fast and slow – and has had procedures designed to restore normal function. But now, he is back to the abnormally slow heart rhythms, and what to do about it is sort of up in the air.

As he sat there telling stories about his life and his dad dying and their relationship, I finally found an opportunity to pop the big question. I asked him if he ever thinks about dying, and, if so, what he thinks about. Here's what he said:

They put me in the hospital one time to do a walking stress test. And I flipped out again – my heart went back into A-fib. So they grabbed me off of that treadmill and put me on a bed, and really started ... paying attention. And they got me past it again. Then, they did a nuclear stress test, where you don't have to exercise.

So, I got out of the hospital and went to see the doctor for the follow-up, and I actually saw him in the hall. He had several doctors who worked with him there – I don't remember which one was supposed to see me – but I was walking down the hall and he passed me, and he says, 'How you doing, Mr. Clark?' I said, 'Well, I'm OK.' He said, 'You better be more than OK.' I said, 'Why is that?' He said, 'When you came to see me, you were a candidate for a heart transplant.'

That woke my brain up.

He was telling me that I was bad off when I went to see him. They said at first that if they couldn't get my heart straightened out, that we'd have to try ... something else. But they also said that they felt like, since I'd been in A-fib for a long time, that my heart was just tired. It was a fast A-fib; the A-fib I'm in now is a slow one. My heart rate is the same as yours. But it just skips around some. It'll be like bong, bong, bong, and then bong, bong, bong-bong. Just all irregular.

Anyway, he got my attention. And so I've thought about that a lot of times, too. But I'm not real concerned about it right now. A-fib is not, in itself, a death sentence. One doctor told me that if you've got to be in A-fib, the slow A-fib is the best one to be in.

But, yeah. I'm real afraid, and scared, of dying. Because I still am not convinced that there is a God. Not totally convinced.

And I've had two instances in my life when I had visions. So, I'm ashamed of myself for not being certain, you know. One time was when Stacy (my oldest daughter) was born. Your mama called me and said that you wanted me to come and give her a blessing. I was gonna go and get somebody from church and take them with me.

Well, I was at home when your mama called me — with no car. Brenda (my sister) was gone with the car. So I was just pacing the floor — 'What am I gonna do; what am I gonna do?' She had said that she (Stacy) was probably going to be blind. So, I was pacing the floor, and all of a sudden, I had the feeling that my mama and daddy were there to comfort me. I mean, they were in that room. I couldn't see them, but I could feel them. And about that time, Brenda drove up and I took off and picked up my friend and we gave Stacy a blessing in the incubator. And the next morning, the doctors said they couldn't believe how much she had improved. They said she would probably have to wear glasses, but she wouldn't be blind. And they couldn't figure out how that had happened. I attribute the blessing for that.

Then, the second time I had a vision, or a feeling, or whatever it was, was when my sister, Nita, called me to tell me that Ruth had died. I hung up the phone and I just shook my head. I bowed my head and I shut my eyes, and I saw a figure, in kind of a mist, facing me, and it looked like my mama. And another figure, with her back to me, that looked like Ruth. And mama was motioning to her, come on. It went away right quick, but during that time, I think I believed there was a God.

I've always been the kind of person who says, 'Show me.' For instance, in my work, when I went to electronics schools and stuff – I'm very mechanical, and if you pour water into a pipe, water comes out the other side. Right? That's logical to me. But in electronics, if you apply an AC power to something, it can come out DC on the other end. And somebody's got to tell me how that works. But nobody can tell you. You just have to accept it, because it works. So I guess that's what I attribute to my doubts about anything. I've got to touch it, see it, feel it.

I do think about it. And what scares me is that I'm afraid that dying is going to be the end of it.

Aunt Nita, who had been napping on and off, suddenly pipes up: *I'm ready any time. I'm ready to go be with Howard.*

I don't like you talking like that, my dad says.

You don't want me telling the truth? Nita says.

Well, just don't say anything, then.

Howard and Nita in their younger years

Older Howard and Nita

All in all, it was a pretty good visit. I heard some stories I'd never heard before, and I enjoyed spending time with my dad and my aunt and stepmom. I was surprised to hear him say he has doubts about God. But that's also kind of cool — that he's not one of these people that talk about "knowing" what's going to happen, because if you ask me, no one knows for certain what happens after we die, because nobody's ever been there and come back to tell the tale. Well, there are near-death experiences out there, but ...

Again, I digress ...

A few years ago, I was hunting through a small file cabinet at home, searching for I don't remember what, when I came across a copy of my birth certificate. I stopped and looked at it. My dad was 21 when I was born, and my mother 20. They lived in a duplex, I think it was, somewhere on Washington Avenue in Houston. Shortly after I came along, they bought their first and only house together: 1,100 square feet, three bedrooms, one bath, on a corner lot in the Langwood subdivision on Houston's northwest side. My dad says my first birthday party was there. I thought about how young they were, and how big a deal it must have been to be having a child and buying a house. I imagined how excited and proud they might have been, and how nervous. A lot of responsibility for a couple of kids barely out of their teens.

And somehow that five minutes of looking at that birth certificate sort of softened my heart for the old man.

I'm not mad at him anymore, like I was for so many years, and I no longer blame him for my screw-ups in life. Those are all on me. I have two daughters and I know for a fact that I have hurt both of them. I didn't mean to, but I did. I've let them both down at different times, and I know I've been a disappointment. I love my girls dearly and would never deliberately do anything to cause them pain, but I have. For no other reason than I'm a human being, and human beings make mistakes. And in spite of it all, my daughters still love me.

Like most parents my old man never meant to hurt me or let me down. I know that now. Like most parents, he did the best he could. He loves me, and I know he is proud of me, in his own way. And I love him.

Back when I was still a newspaper reporter, I was getting restless and considering making a career move, trying to do something else for a living. I was thinking about becoming a school teacher, but couldn't really see myself standing up in front of a classroom full of kids. I'm a big-time introvert and don't like the spotlight on me at all. Everyone I talked to about it, though, said they thought I'd make a good teacher. And then I talked to a woman I knew who was a deputy superintendent for one of the local school districts. I knew her from covering city council meetings and school board meetings and such, so I called and made an appointment to see her. We sat down next to each other in a conference room, and I explained why I was there and that I would like her opinion.

"I think you'd make a great teacher," she said.

"What makes you say that?" I asked.

"Because ... you're a good man."

I got a lump in my throat and felt tears coming up. I told myself, don't you dare start crying. We talked a little more, and then I thanked her and we shook hands and I left. And my decision was made. I enrolled in a teacher certification program, and I've now been a teacher for 13 years.

To me, being a good man is the highest compliment. It's the ultimate. And I think my dad is a good man. A little too self-centered, maybe, but, hell, so am I. I'm not sure if that trait is genetically inherited, or a learned behavior. But we're a lot alike in that way, and in others.

He's a good man.

~~~~~~~

Me and Granddaddy

Nita holding me; my mother, Billie Jo, and Maa-Maw

Me and my dad

Get My Books FREE

Visit my website www.johnclarkbooks.com, and subscribe to my mailing list to get all of my new releases for free. I plan to write many books over the coming years, and I'd love to repay you for taking an interest in my work by allowing you to access all of my future work at no charge. When each new book is released, I'll send you an email with a link to the free book. No strings attached and nothing for sale ever. Subscribe today at: www.johnclarkbooks.com

A Small Favor to Ask

Thanks for reading this collection; I hope you found these stories meaningful or helpful in some way. If you did, please take just a moment to write a brief review on Amazon of it. Your reviews mean a great deal to me, and they help others find this book, so that more readers can read these stories and perhaps find some resonance with their own experience, and answers of their own.

About the Author

John Henry Clark III is an award-winning journalist, freelance writer, author and avid golfer who was born and raised in Texas. He grew up in northwest Houston playing sports at Oaks Dads Club and attending church with his parents, but decided as he got older that things he learned in Sunday school no longer made much sense.

Since then, he has spent a lifetime seeking answers and exploring a variety of beliefs. After a successful career as a newspaper reporter, Clark turned his lifetime love for learning into a new career as a public school teacher, and that gave him time during the summer months to pursue his project to research and write a book describing what people believe about God and why they believe what they believe.

That effort turned into the book, *Finding God: An Exploration of Spiritual Diversity in America's Heartland*. A tireless seeker, researcher and questioner, John has written a number of other fascinating books dealing with the human experience, from tragedies to triumphs and more, including *Camino: Laughter and Tears along Spain's 500-mile Camino de Santiago*. To read more of John's books, find answers to the meaning of life, and maybe discover something new about yourself, go here: http://amzn.to/1EmgWa7

Manufactured by Amazon.ca
Acheson, AB